# Wallace & Gromit

## A MATTER OF LOAF AND DEATH
## JOKE BOOK

Jokes by
Penny Worms

Screenplay by
Nick Park and Bob Baker

First published in Great Britain 2008
by Egmont UK Limited
239 Kensington High Street, London W8 6SA

ISBN 978 1 4052 4447 3
1 3 5 7 9 10 8 6 4 2

Printed in Italy

# CONTENTS

# TOP BUN'S TOP THIRTY BAKER JOKES

Wallace and Gromit are the proud owners of a new bakery business, Top Bun. They have converted their house into a working windmill, where they bake the finest bread, buns and cakes in town.

They deliver their produce in the Top Bun van, and like to make their customers smile with a joke a day.

*Here are some of their favourites . . .*

Why are bakers
so cruel?

Because they beat
the eggs and whip
the cream.

Why did the baker stop
making doughnuts?

He got tired of the
hole thing.

What's the difference
between bread and
the sun?

The sun rises from
the east. Bread rises
from the yeast.

There once was a baker
who was six feet tall,
had a huge tummy
and size 11 feet.
What did he weigh?
Flour.

Did you hear
about the baker
who thought
that shortbread
was made by
cutting a
French stick
in half?

Did you hear the joke about the butter? I'd better not tell you. You might spread it.

Which is the most filling kind of bread? WHOLEMEAL.

HEE HEE! HA HA! HEE HEE!

Why did the pie go to the dentist?

Because it needed a filling.

How do you interrogate toast?

Give it a good grilling.

Two muffins are baking in the oven. One says, "Wow, it's hot in here!"

The other replies, "Cripes! A talking muffin!"

What kind of garden does a baker have?

A flour garden.

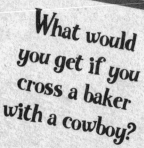

What would you get if you cross a baker with a cowboy?

Someone who goes in all buns glazing.

HEE HEE! HA HA! HEE HEE!

Why did the baker work such long hours?

Because he kneaded the dough.

Why did the cookies go bad?

Because they were made with a mould.

Why is bun number six afraid of bun number seven?

Because seven eight nine.

How do you make an apple crumble?
Hit it with a hammer.

How do you make a swiss roll?

Throw it down a hill.

HEE HEE! HA HA! HEE HEE!

How do you make a cream puff? Chase it up a hill.

Why do bakers need
an alarm clock?

Their loaves
can't rise without one.

How do you
make a
cake stand?

Take its chair away.

Who goes undercover
in a bakery at
Christmas?

A mince spy.

## What's Egyptian pie?

The type of pie that mummy used to make.

## Why were the two currants so happy?

They were on a roll.

Why did the loaf rise to the occasion?

It was the yeast it could do.

How do you know if a baker is sad?

Even his cakes are in tiers.

HEE HEE! HA HA! HEE HEE!

Bakers trade bread recipes on a knead to know basis.

What did the baker's hat say to his apron?

"You hang around, I'll go on a head."

What did the poorly baker say to the doctor?

"I'm sick of my-grains."

What do bakers use to make fairy cakes?

Elf-raising flour.

HO HO!

HEH
HEH HEH ...

What's another name for an onion bagel?

A bun-ion.

# GOING TO THE BAKERY...

If you went into the Top Bun bakery, what would you buy?

What would a monkey buy?

Banana bread.

# What would a mouse buy?

Cheesecake.

# What would a rabbit buy?

Carrot cake.

# WHAT WOULD A GRANDMOTHER BUY?

## NAAN BREAD.

What would an orang-utan buy?

Gingerbread.

What would an electrician buy?

A currant bun.

HEE HEE! HA HA! HEE HEE!

**What would a saucer buy?**

A cupcake.

**What would a plumber buy?**

A Bath bun.

**Why should bakers be above sarcasm?**

Because it's the lowest form of wheat.

**What happened when the cake tried to become a movie star?**

It got panned by the critics.

What's the only way Gromit can get breakfast in bed?

To sleep in the kitchen.

How do you pay for a bag of buns?

With currantsy.

# WALLACE'S FINEST JOKES

Wallace the cheese-loving inventor likes to tell Gromit a good joke or two when they're out on their rounds.

## Unfortunately for Gromit,

Wallace doesn't know any good jokes!

Here are some of
his latest ones . . .

What starts with a T,
ends in a T and contains
lots of lovely T? A teapot.

HA HA!
HA HA!

What do you get if you mix a lot of dough with a fiddle?

A-bun-dance.

What's the most embarrassing thing you can buy in a bakery?

Bloomers.

30

HEE HEE! HA HA!

What birds can you buy in a bakery?

Bay-gulls.

31

Why did the baker make cat-shaped biscuits?

He wanted to sell crumb-pets.

Why did none of the crumb-pets sell?

Because it was a half-baked idea.

One of my faves, eh, lad!

HA!

Now, what do you think of this?
If you scoff all my cakes, what's left for me?

Muffin! Get it?

What did the farmhouse loaf say when it got squashed?

"Don't worry, I'm all-white."

Thought you'd like that one!

Why did the baker flip?

Because he saw the apple turnover.

What do you call an old baker's van?

A crust bucket.

What are the perfect pastries for a tea dance?

Raisin twists and cinnamon whirls.

How do you tell if a baker is enlightened?

He understands the meaning of loaf.

A little boy walked into a bakery. "Do you sell fishcakes?" he asked.

The baker replied: "This is a bakery, sonny, not a fish and chip shop."

The little boy started to cry. "But I wanted a cake for my fish. It's his birthday!"

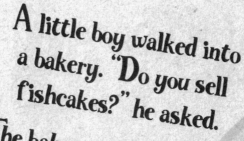

35

# JOKES THAT MAKE GROMIT LAUGH

After a hard day's work in the bakery, Gromit likes to relax with a good book.

One of his favourites is Howling Good Dog Jokes, by Al Satian.

Here are some of his favourites . . .

# Which dogs are the cleanest?

Shampoodles.

# Which dog is most useful in the kitchen?

A cooker spaniel.

# What is the only dog you should eat?

A hot-dog.

Which composer do dogs like best?

Bach.

Why did the dog run into a corner every time the doorbell rang?

Because he was a boxer.

What do you need to make dog biscuits?

Collie flour.

When it's raining cats and dogs, be careful not to tread in a poodle.

HA HA!
HA HA!

# INTRODUCING FLUFFLES

Fluffles is a little poodle with a big heart. She is mistreated by her mad, murdering mistress, Piella Bakewell, but still keeps her sense of humour. Her favourite jokes are shaggy-dog stories about clever dogs and silly humans.

Two friends are watching an Agatha Christie film on TV. One of them has a dog, that growls whenever the villain appears and wags his tail whenever the hero comes on. The second friend says to the dog owner: "That's extraordinary behaviour for a dog."
"You're right," says the owner. "It's surprising because he hated the book."

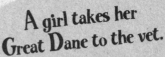

A girl takes her Great Dane to the vet.

"My dog's cross-eyed. Is there anything you can do for him?" she said.

"Well," says the vet, "let's have a look at him." So he picks up the dog and examines his eyes, then checks his teeth. Finally, he says, "I'm going to have to put this dog down."

"What!?" cries the girl. "Because he's cross-eyed?"

"No, because he's really heavy."

In the park, a man came across a boy playing chess with his dog. Astonished, the man says: "What a clever dog!" The boy replies: "No, no, he isn't that clever. I'm leading by three games to one!"

— ● ● ● —

Two gas men need to make some repairs to a house, but the sign on the gate says: DANGER! BEWARE OF DOG! One of the men refuses to go in, but the other man is brave and he likes dogs, so he carefully opens the gate. He sees an old sausage dog snoozing on the path. The dog's elderly owner is in the garden pruning his roses. "So THAT's the dangerous dog!" the gas man scoffs. He calls to his mate to ignore the sign. As his mate walks into the garden he trips over the dog and bashes his head on the path. "See," says the old man, "I warned you he was dangerous."

HA HA!

A dog goes for a job with M15. The M15 agent looks at the dog and says, "I don't think this job is for you, you've got to be able to type." The dog jumps up to the computer and types 60 words in a minute. Then he has to complete an obstacle course within 90 seconds. The dog crosses the line in 40. Next, the dog has to pick out the spy from a 10-man line-up. There are a number of clues on the table, but the dog uses his sense of smell to find the culprit.

Impressed, the M15 agent says: "There's one final requirement. You must be bilingual." The dog looks up at the agent, cocks his head to one side and says:

"Miaow!"

# INTRODUCING PIELLA, THE BAKE-O-NOT-SO-LITE GIRL

Piella used to be the beautiful Bake-O-Lite girl, the face of Bake-O-Lite slimmer's bread. But over the years, she ate too many rolls and now she has too many rolls on her! She's been sacked and now she's intent on revenge.

**What does Gromit think of Piella?**

That she's barking mad.

**Why does Piella like biscuits?**

Because she's crackers.

**Why does Piella like pecan pie?**

Because she's completely nutty.

Why is Piella like
a candle?

They're both wicked.

Why should Piella
never ride a bike?

Because she's always
flying off the handle.

How does Piella keep
her hair in place?

With scare spray.

46

What are Piella's
two favourite
foods?

I-scream and batter.

How did Piella
mark her
engagement
to Baker Bob?

With a celebratory
bash.

# IT'S A MATTER OF LOAF AND DEATH

The headlines of the The Daily Grind make grim reading for all those in the bakery business. A twelfth baker has been killed, battered to death with his own rolling pin. Gromit is worried but Wallace always likes to look on the bright side.

Nothing like a joke to make light of a sinister situation . . .

When the police are called to the scene of a crime, the detective asks what's happened.

The sergeant replies: "There's a man over there covered in cornflakes and he's dead."

"That's odd," says the detective. "Didn't we have one covered in muesli yesterday? And another covered in rice puffs last week?"

"Yes," says the sergeant. "The cereal killer has struck again."

49

## How do Fluffles and Gromit meet?

When Fluffles is about to meet her baker.

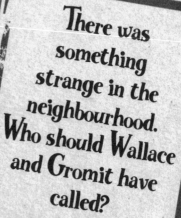

There was something strange in the neighbourhood. Who should Wallace and Gromit have called?

Toastbusters.

HEE HEE! HA HA! HEE HEE!

How does Gromit
save Fluffles?
He uses his loaf.

Hee hee! Ha ha! Hee hee! Ha ha! Ha ha! Hee hee!

Why does Piella kill her boyfriends?

She likes to chop and change.

HEE HEE! HA HA! HEE HEE!

52

What do you call Piella when she's flying?

A balloonatic.

HEE HEE! HA HA! HEE HEE!

What's the difference between Wallace and Piella?

One makes cake batters, the other batters cake-makers.

Why is Wallace such a lazy baker?

He can't stop loafing about.

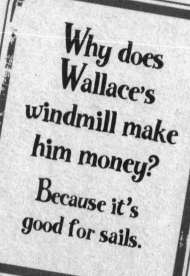

Why does Wallace's windmill make him money?

Because it's good for sails.

HEE HEE! HA HA! HEE HEE! HA HA!

**Why is Gromit such a good baker?**

Because he's well-bread.

How does Gromit feel when Wallace makes him clean the plates?

All washed up.

HEE HEE! HA HA! HEE HEE!

Why doesn't Gromit refuse to do all the baking single-handed?

It would go against the grain of his nature.

How does Wallace slow down Piella's bicycle?

He puts the cakes on.

HA HA! HA HA!

HEE HEE! HA HA! HEE HEE! HA HA!

Why does Fluffles leave Piella?

Because their relationship goes stale.

Hee hee! Ha ha! Hee hee! Ha ha! Hee hee! Ha ha! Ha ha!

Why is Gromit good at making shortbread?

Because he doesn't waffle on.

HA-HA!

HA-HA!

Why does
Piella sink her teeth
into her own arm?

To put the bite
on Gromit.

HEE HEE! HA HA! HEE HEE!

How does Wallace
react to Gromit's
warnings about Piella?

He turns a chef ear.

## Why do Wallace and Gromit open a bakery?

Because they need to earn a crust.

## What do you call a string of bakers dangling over a crocodile pit in summer?

A hot cross bungee.

Why do Wallace's trousers shock the nuns?
Because they're holey.

What happens at the end of
A Matter of Loaf and Death?

Piella gets her just
desserts . . .

And Fluffles joining
Top Bun is a change for
the batter !

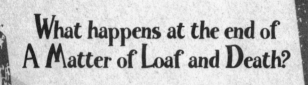